Ruth Bader Ginsburg

SUPREME COURT JUSTICE

by Meg Gaertner

FOCUS READERS.

BEACON

www.focusreaders.com

Copyright © 2021 by Focus Readers®, Lake Elmo, MN 55042. All rights reserved. No part of this book may be reproduced or utilized in any form or by any means without written permission from the publisher.

Focus Readers is distributed by North Star Editions: sales@northstareditions.com | 888-417-0195

Produced for Focus Readers by Red Line Editorial.

Photographs ©: Ron Edmonds/AP Images, cover, 1; Marcy Nighswander/AP Images, 4; Ken Heinen/AP Images, 7; Doug Mills/AP Images, 8, 19; Shutterstock Images, 11, 13, 14, 17; J. Scott Applewhite/AP Images, 20–21; Rapport Press/Newscom, 22, 29; Max Oden/Sipa USA/AP Images, 25; Pablo Martinez Monsivais/AP Images, 27

Library of Congress Cataloging-in-Publication Data
Names: Gaertner, Meg, author.
Title: Ruth Bader Ginsburg : Supreme Court Justice / by Meg Gaertner.
Description: Lake Elmo, MN : Focus Readers, [2021] | Series: Important
  women | Includes index. | Audience: Grades 4-6
Identifiers: LCCN 2020033539 (print) | LCCN 2020033540 (ebook) | ISBN
  9781644936870 (hardcover) | ISBN 9781644937235 (paperback) | ISBN
  9781644937952 (pdf) | ISBN 9781644937594 (ebook)
Subjects: LCSH: Ginsburg, Ruth Bader--Juvenile literature. | Women
  judges--United States--Biography--Juvenile literature. | Judges--United
  States--Biography--Juvenile literature. | United States. Supreme
  Court--Officials and employees--Biography--Juvenile literature.
Classification: LCC KF8745.G56 G34 2021 (print) | LCC KF8745.G56 (ebook)
  | DDC 347.73/2634 [B]--dc23
LC record available at https://lccn.loc.gov/2020033539
LC ebook record available at https://lccn.loc.gov/2020033540

Printed in the United States of America
Mankato, MN
012021

About the Author

Meg Gaertner is a children's book editor and writer. She lives in Minneapolis, where she enjoys swing dancing and spending time outside. She is grateful for the opportunities she has, and for the important women whose groundbreaking work made those opportunities possible.

Table of Contents

Chapter 1

Becoming a Justice

In 1993, there was a spot to fill on the US **Supreme Court**. President Bill Clinton chose Ruth Bader Ginsburg as the new **justice**. Ginsburg had worked in law for many years.

Ginsburg takes an oath to become a Supreme Court justice in 1993.

On August 10, Ginsburg stood in the White House. She raised her right hand. She promised to defend the US Constitution. This document lays out the basic beliefs and laws of the United States. The crowd clapped. Cameras flashed. Ginsburg was now a justice.

Did You Know?

Sandra Day O'Connor was the first female justice. She served on the Supreme Court from 1981 to 2006.

 President Bill Clinton (center) visits the Supreme Court in October 1993.

The Supreme Court had existed for more than 200 years. In all that time, Ginsburg was only the second woman to join it. As a justice, she would help decide many important legal cases.

Chapter 2

Overcoming Challenges

Joan Ruth Bader was born on March 15, 1933. She grew up in New York City. Joan began to go by "Ruth" as a child. Her father sold goods. Her mother worked in a factory.

 Like her mother, Ruth (center) worked and raised a family at the same time.

School was very important to Ruth and her mother. This belief was uncommon at the time. Most people thought women should not do certain things. Ruth disagreed. She would spend her life working to change these limits. But her mother did not get to see Ruth's success.

Did You Know?

The Baders were Jewish. The family attended a synagogue when Ruth was growing up.

 Women in the 1930s protest being overlooked for jobs.

She died right before Ruth finished high school.

Ruth left New York City to go to college. She chose to study at Cornell University. She won a **scholarship**. And in 1954, she finished at the top of her class.

That same year, she married Martin Ginsburg. She took his last name. She became Ruth Bader Ginsburg.

Ginsburg started a family. Then she entered Harvard Law School in 1956. That year, her husband learned he had cancer. Ginsburg cared for him and their daughter. She studied law at the same time.

Did You Know?

Ginsburg's class at Harvard had 500 people. She was one of only nine women.

Columbia University has one of the top law schools in the entire world.

Ginsburg's husband got better. He moved to New York City for work. Ginsburg went with him. She finished her studies at Columbia Law School. She graduated at the top of her class in 1959.

Chapter 3

Feminist Icon

Ginsburg was very successful at school. Even so, she struggled to find work. People **discriminated** against her. At the time, very few women were lawyers. And many places chose to hire only men.

 As a judge and lawyer, Ginsburg worked to protect people from discrimination.

In 1963, Ginsburg began teaching law at Rutgers University. She stayed there until 1972. Then she taught at Columbia. She was the first woman to earn a long-term teaching job there.

Ginsburg also worked with the American Civil Liberties Union

Did You Know?

Rutgers wanted to pay Ginsburg less than male teachers. She went to court. She won the case and got equal pay.

 Ginsburg helped the ACLU argue several cases before the Supreme Court.

(ACLU). This group works to guard people's rights. Ginsburg helped the ACLU on several cases. One case focused on a law in Idaho. The law discriminated against women. Ginsburg argued against the state's law. She said it was illegal.

Ginsburg pointed out that the Constitution promises **equal protection**. She said that idea applies to women, too.

The US Supreme Court agreed. It declared Idaho's law illegal. For the first time, the court had ruled against gender discrimination.

In 1972, Ginsburg formed the Women's Rights Project. This part of the ACLU fights for gender equality. Throughout the 1970s, Ginsburg argued six cases before

 Ginsburg stands in her office at the US Court of Appeals for the District of Columbia Circuit.

the Supreme Court. She won five of them. She became known as an **advocate** for equal rights.

In 1980, Ginsburg left Columbia. She worked on a US **Court of Appeals** for 13 years. Then in 1993, she joined the Supreme Court.

Dissenting Decisions

To decide a Supreme Court case, a majority of justices must agree. But justices can **dissent**. In 2006, for instance, a woman **sued** the company she worked for. She had the same skills as male workers. But she was paid much less. The Supreme Court ruled against the woman. It said she was too late. A law gave people a limited amount of time to sue.

Ginsburg dissented. She thought the court misunderstood the law. She asked Congress to change the law. It did. In 2009, a new law gave workers more time to sue.

Ginsburg wore different collars to show if she agreed or dissented.

Chapter 4

On the Court

As a justice, Ginsburg heard many cases. She kept defending equal rights. Sometimes her view won. One example was a case about a military program. In 1996, the program was accepting only men.

Ginsburg wrote several famous rulings and dissents.

Ginsburg said this was illegal. Women should be able to enter the program, too. Six other justices agreed with her.

In other cases, she dissented. In 2013, the Supreme Court ended part of the Voting Rights Act. This decision made it easier for states to change their voting laws. Ginsburg

Ginsburg was known for her dissents. She had a nickname: "Notorious R.B.G."

 Ginsburg became so well known that a company made action figures of her.

did not support it. She feared states would limit people's right to vote.

Another example took place in 2014. A law required companies to pay for part of workers' health care.

But some companies didn't want to pay. They said the law went against their religious beliefs.

The Supreme Court ruled that these companies could refuse to pay. Ginsburg disagreed. She felt the court's decision was dangerous. It could let companies force their beliefs on workers. Or, it could help companies try to argue that they didn't need to follow other laws.

Ginsburg worked until her death in September 2020. She was 87.

 Sonia Sotomayor (back left) and Elena Kagan (back right) joined the Supreme Court by 2010.

She had battled cancer for many years. People honored Ginsburg's life and work. They remembered her as a fighter for gender equality. And they promised to continue the work she had begun.

Ruth Bader Ginsburg

Write your answers on a separate piece of paper.

1. Write a paragraph describing one case in which Ginsburg dissented.

2. Which of Ginsburg's successes do you think is the most impressive? Why?

3. When did Ginsburg join the US Supreme Court?
- A. 1972
- B. 1993
- C. 2014

4. How might Ginsburg's work experiences have shaped her views on gender equality?
- A. She learned that people are always treated equally.
- B. She discovered that women don't learn as well as men.
- C. She experienced discrimination herself.

5. What does **graduated** mean in this book?

*She finished her studies at Columbia Law School. She **graduated** at the top of her class in 1959.*

    A. argued a case in court

    B. completed a program of study

    C. failed to complete a program

6. What does **ruled** mean in this book?

*The Supreme Court **ruled** that these companies could refuse to pay. Ginsburg disagreed. She felt the court's decision was dangerous.*

    A. measured with a ruler

    B. had power over a country

    C. made a decision in a case

Answer key on page 32.

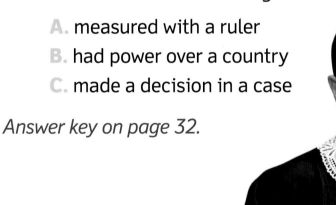

Glossary

advocate
A person who supports a specific idea.

court of appeals
A court that decides whether the law was correctly applied in lower-level courts.

discriminated
Treated others unfairly because of who they are or how they look.

dissent
To disagree with the court's decision.

equal protection
The idea that states must rule fairly and protect citizens equally under the law.

justice
A person who hears cases in a court of law, especially in the Supreme Court.

scholarship
Money given to a student to pay for education expenses.

sued
Took legal action against a person or group.

Supreme Court
The highest court of law in the United States.

To Learn More

BOOKS

Alkire, Jessie. *Ruth Bader Ginsburg*. Minneapolis: Abdo Publishing, 2020.

Micklos, John, Jr. *Ruth Bader Ginsburg: Get to Know the Justice Who Speaks Her Mind*. North Mankato, MN: Capstone Press, 2019.

Tyner, Artika R. *So You Want to Be a Supreme Court Justice*. North Mankato, MN: Capstone Press, 2020.

NOTE TO EDUCATORS

Visit **www.focusreaders.com** to find lesson plans, activities, links, and other resources related to this title.

Index

A
American Civil Liberties Union (ACLU), 16–18

C
Columbia Law School, 13, 16, 19

D
dissent, 20, 24

H
Harvard Law School, 12

O
O'Connor, Sandra Day, 6

R
Rutgers University, 16

U
US Constitution, 6, 18
US Court of Appeals, 19
US Supreme Court, 5–7, 18–19, 20, 24, 26

V
Voting Rights Act, 24

W
Women's Rights Project, 18

Answer Key: 1. Answers will vary; **2.** Answers will vary; **3.** B; **4.** C; **5.** B; **6.** C